Searchlight BOOKS

Predators

Polar Bears
on the Hunt

Meg Marquardt

Lerner Publications • Minneapolis

Content Consultant: Tom Smith, PhD, Associate Professor and Research Wildlife
Biologist, Department of Plant and Wildlife Sciences, Brigham Young University

Lerner Publications Company
A division of Lerner Publishing Group, Inc.
241 First Avenue North
Minneapolis, MN 55401 USA

For reading levels and more information, look up this title at
www.lernerbooks.com.

Library of Congress Cataloging-in-Publication Data

Names: Marquardt, Meg, author.
Title: Polar bears on the hunt / Meg Marquardt.
Description: Minneapolis : Lerner Publications, [2018] | Series: Searchlight books.
    Predators | Audience: Ages 8–11. | Audience: Grades 4 to 6. | Includes bibliographical
    references and index.
Identifiers: LCCN 2017019986 (print) | LCCN 2017004829 (ebook) | ISBN 9781512450828
    (eb pdf) | ISBN 9781512433975 (lb : alk. paper) | ISBN 9781512456110 (pb : alk. paper)
Subjects: LCSH: Polar bear—Juvenile literature. | Predatory animals—Juvenile literature. |
    Predation (Biology)—Juvenile literature.
Classification: LCC QL737.C27 (print) | LCC QL737.C27 M34585 2018 (ebook) | DDC
    599.786—dc23

LC record available at https://lccn.loc.gov/2017019986

Manufactured in the United States of America
1 — CG — 7/15/17

Contents

Chapter 1

ON THE HUNT . . . **page 4**

Chapter 2

LIVING ON THE ICE . . . **page 9**

Chapter 3

MADE FOR THE COLD . . . **page 15**

Chapter 4

POLAR BEAR BEHAVIOR . . . **page 21**

Polar Bear Fact File • 28
Glossary • 30
Learn More about Polar Bears • 31
Index • 32

ON THE HUNT

A polar bear prowls across the ice. Even though he weighs as much as two vending machines, he is quiet above the ice. However, underneath the ice, it's a different story. To a ringed seal, a polar bear's footsteps sound like thunder. The ice cracks a little with each heavy step. When a polar bear is on the move, a seal knows to stay out of sight.

Polar bears usually hunt on sea ice. How loud are their footsteps above ice?

This polar bear is looking for a hole in the ice. Seals need to surface to breathe approximately every fifteen minutes. They cut large holes in the ice with the claws on their flippers. They use the holes to pop up for air. The polar bear finds one of these holes. It waits for the best time to strike. The bear waits for hours. But no seal comes up for air at this spot.

▲
A POLAR BEAR WAITS BY A HOLE
FOR A SEAL TO SURFACE.

Ringed seals come up to the ice to rest after a dive.

A New Strategy

The bear is hungry, and he has not eaten in a week. He tries a new strategy. He catches sight of a ringed seal in the distance. The seal has surfaced to sleep and bask in the sun. The bear drops down to his belly. He crawls slowly toward the seal, stalking it. The seal raises its head every so often to look for predators. When the seal does this, the bear freezes. Since the bear's coat blends in with the ice and snow, the seal does not see it.

The bear is 20 feet (6 meters) away. He is ready for the final strike. With a mighty lunge, he races across the ice. Out of the water, the seal cannot make a quick escape. Using his powerful jaws, the bear catches the seal.

Seals are a high-energy food source for polar bears.

One Big Feast

When seals are plentiful, polar bears eat only the fat. They leave the rest of the meat, and other predators like foxes and birds eat it. However, during the summer there is less ice, and it is not as easy to find seals. When seals are scarce, polar bears eat their meat too. Rarely, polar bears eat whatever they can find, sometimes birds or bird eggs. Pregnant females in the Hudson Bay area can go as long as eight months without food.

Birds may finish eating what a polar bear leaves behind.

Chapter 2

LIVING ON THE ICE

Polar bears thrive in the cold. They live in the Arctic and subarctic regions. The Arctic covers the northernmost part of the globe. The subarctic is just south of it. That means polar bears live in many countries. There are polar bears in Russia, Greenland, Norway, the United States, and Canada. About 60 to 80 percent of all polar bears live in Canada.

Some polar bears spend the summer months on icebergs when the sea ice has melted. Which countries do polar bears live in?

There are about 22,000 to 31,000 polar bears worldwide. It is tricky to guess their exact numbers, because polar bears live far away from people. Some even live close to the North Pole. The places they live are cold and far from cities or towns, making research difficult and dangerous. And polar bears tend to be solitary. It is hard to find one bear in a giant, icy plain.

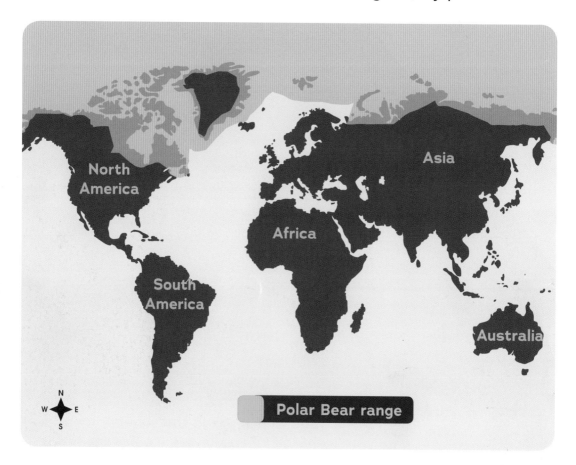

Polar Bear range

At Home on Ice

Because polar bears live in the cold North, their habitat is mostly ice and snow. They spend a majority or all of their time on sea ice, which covers the Arctic region. Seals, the bears' main prey, swim under the ice and surface for air.

During the summer months, polar bears move farther north to escape the heat. If the sea ice melts completely, they may live on northern coasts, including those of Canada or Alaska. But they always return to the sea ice. They will swim for long distances to find it.

Polar bears' scientific Latin name is _Ursus maritimus_, or sea bear.

Polar bears are considered a vulnerable species. This means they are in danger of going extinct, which would be a big problem for the Arctic ecosystem. Polar bears are the apex predators in the region. Without them to control populations, too many seals may overfeed on fish, which keep other species populations in check. Apex predators are needed to keep an ecosystem healthy and balanced.

Polar bears help control the ecosystem by eating seals. If polar bears die out, the seal population would grow, and the ecosystem would be out of balance.

A bear eats a jar of dressing at a dump in Canada. Polar bears may look for food at landfills when sea ice melts and prey becomes scarce.

The biggest threat to polar bears is rapidly melting sea ice. Climate change threatens polar bears' lives. They use the ice to hunt. Polar bears that live farthest south are spending up to six months on land. Each year, the ice melts earlier in the spring and re-forms later in the fall. This forces polar bears to find different food sources, such as human trash. This food is unhealthy for the bears, and it is dangerous to have bears living so close to humans. If the ice continues to melt, polar bears will be in trouble.

Finding New Food

Without sea ice, polar bears cannot hunt for seals and have to find other food sources. They will then eat snow geese and their eggs, which creates problems. Birds and eggs do not have enough fat for polar bears to live on. The bears are also wiping out whole colonies of birds. This can cause big disruptions in the ecosystem.

Birds are not big enough nor are there enough of them to be a polar bear's main food source.

Chapter 3

MADE FOR THE COLD

The polar bear is the largest land predator on the planet. A large male polar bear can weigh up to 1,763 pounds (800 kilograms). A female can be up to 1,000 pounds (454 kg). When it's walking on all fours, a polar bear can be almost as tall as a refrigerator at the shoulder: up to 5.6 feet (1.7 m). If a bear rears back to stand on its hind legs, it can be nearly 13 feet (4 m) tall.

Polar bears stand on their hind legs to get a better look at something. How tall can they be when standing on their hind legs?

A polar bear's white fur makes it hard for prey to spot it on the ice.

Winter Coat

These big bears are masters of adaptation. They have to be. In some regions of the Arctic, the sun does not rise from October through February. Temperatures can drop lower than -50°F (-46°C).

Fur is one of a polar bear's most important adaptations to the Arctic. A polar bear's fur may look white, but it is actually clear and hollow. When light strikes a piece of fur, the light is reflected back. When light is fully reflected, the object it scatters off of looks white.

Underneath that fur is a layer of dark black skin. That black can be seen on the nose, lips, tongue, and paw pads. Black skin is essential for keeping the polar bear warm. The color absorbs more warmth from the sun's rays.

Beneath the skin is a polar bear's best protection against the cold: fat. Polar bears can have fat as thick as 4.5 inches (11.4 centimeters). It helps keep the bear's body heat inside. Since polar bears swim a lot, fat is especially important. Fat keeps polar bears from freezing on long ocean journeys. It also helps polar bears float.

Some polar bears' tongues are mostly black, while others are pink and black.

Hunting Aids

Polar bears have a second eyelid called a nictitating membrane. When a polar bear is in the water, this thin, clear lid slides down over the eye. The nictitating membrane helps protect the eye from seawater.

To survive in the Arctic, the bears have adapted senses that make them effective hunters. Their sense of smell is especially sharp. They can smell a seal miles away.

The nictitating membrane protects a polar bear's eyes from sunlight in addition to seawater.

A polar bear's paws are essential to its survival in the Arctic.

A polar bear's paws have adapted to icy living too. One paw measures up to 12 inches (31 cm) across. A big paw means the polar bear's weight is more spread out. This helps the bear walk over thin ice without breaking it.

The paw pads are also bumpy. These bumps act like no-slip grips on the ice. But if the ice is too slippery, the bear can use its claws. A polar bear's claws can be up to 2 inches (5.1 cm) long. If a polar bear starts to slide, it digs in its claws to stop itself.

A Polar Bear Dives Deep

Webbed feet make polar bears great swimmers. Typically, though, they only dive for up to thirty seconds. However, researchers timed one bear for much longer in 2015. While stalking seals lounging on an ice floe, the polar bear dove under the surface and swam toward them. After the three-minute-and-ten-second-long underwater swim, it burst onto the floe in a sneak attack.

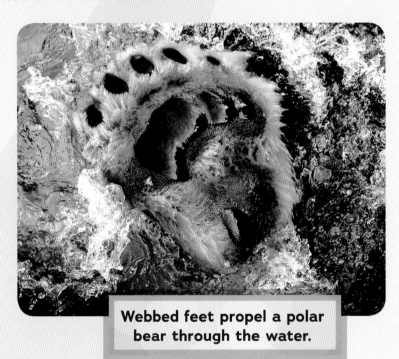

Webbed feet propel a polar bear through the water.

Chapter 4

POLAR BEAR BEHAVIOR

Polar bears live mostly solitary lives, though they are not generally aggressive toward other bears. They come together during mating season, which takes place in late spring or early summer. A male locates a female by using his excellent nose to follow her scent. After the male leaves, he may try to find another female to mate with.

Polar bears usually stay together for a week when mating. How do they find a mate?

If there is not enough sea ice, a female may not be able to gain enough weight to have cubs.

The female is on her own for the rest of her pregnancy. A fertilized egg does not grow right away. A pregnant female must be ready to care for cubs. This means she has to find enough to eat. She will gain around 450 pounds (204 kg) before she gives birth. Bear cubs also need to be born during the right time of year. Winter is when chances of survival are the highest, because the mother has stored up extra fat. If a female's fat stores are high enough in autumn, the egg finally starts growing into a fetus.

Mothers dig dens in the snow to birth their young. Dens protect them from wind and the cold of winter. The den can be more than 40°F (4.4°C) warmer inside than the outside temperature. The den also helps the mother protect her cubs from predators, including male polar bears. By late December or early January, the cubs arrive. Typically, a litter consists of two cubs. Even though polar bears are the biggest land predators, their babies are small, weighing around 1 pound (0.5 kg). They nurse up to six times a day and grow quickly.

Cubs play to develop necessary survival skills.

Walking Hibernation

Unlike other bears, polar bears do not hibernate. Some researchers once thought they entered a state called walking hibernation. Scientists thought polar bears could slow their metabolism when food is scarce during the summer. With a slower metabolism, bears would need less food to function. However, research in 2015 disproved this theory. Pregnant females do dig a den and live off their fat. But their heart rate and temperature do not drop as they would in true hibernation.

Only pregnant polar bears dig dens.

The Polar Bear Life Cycle

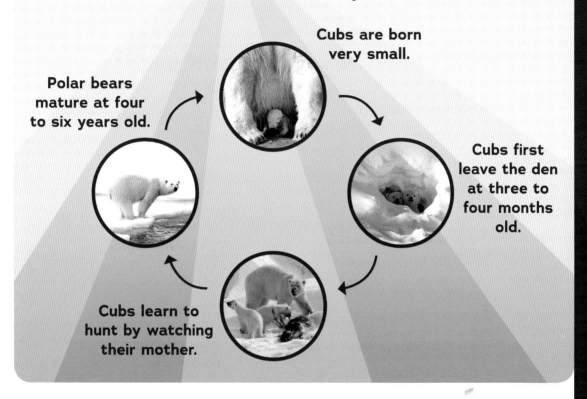

Cubs are born very small.

Polar bears mature at four to six years old.

Cubs first leave the den at three to four months old.

Cubs learn to hunt by watching their mother.

In spring, the cubs begin exploring the world. They can weigh up to 20 pounds (9 kg), but they still depend on their mother. They drink their mother's milk and stay with her for up to two years before she or a male chases them off. The life cycle begins again when the bears are old enough to reproduce, between four and six years old. Polar bears live for up to twenty-five years in the wild.

Communication

Even though polar bears are mostly solitary, they still have ways to communicate with each other. They will shake their heads from side to side if they want to play. Adult males often pretend to fight to practice their hunting skills. If they want to attack, they will drop their heads and pin back their ears. They may growl, hiss, or snort. Two males may fight over a female during breeding season.

Polar bears also communicate with scent. Their feet leave a scent that can tell other bears their gender. If a bear is a female, the scent may tell if she is ready to breed.

Play fighting helps polar bears sharpen their hunting skills.

Polar bears spar over a whale carcass.

Fights may also break out over food. However, polar bears will sometimes share food. If one bear finds another eating a large seal or even a whale, it will circle the meal. The newcomer will touch its nose to the other bear's nose. If all goes well, they will share the meal.

However, after the food is gone, the polar bears will part ways. Polar bears are lone hunters. They prowl the ice looking for their next meal. With their Arctic adaptations, no other animal can top the abilities of these predators of the ice.

POLAR BEAR

Fact File

Scientific Name: *Ursus maritimus*

Where It Is Found: the Arctic and subarctic North, including Russia, Canada, Greenland, Norway, and the United States

Habitat: sea ice, Arctic coastal regions

Diet: seals, walruses, whale carcasses, birds, bird eggs

Height: 3.5 to 5.6 feet (1–1.7 m) tall at the shoulder, up to 13 feet (4 m) when standing on hind legs

Length: 7.25 to 8 feet (2.2–2.4 m)

Weight: Males weigh 775 to 1,763 pounds (352–800 kg). Females weigh 330 to 650 pounds (150–295 kg).

Life Span: up to 25 years in the wild

Food Chain

Glossary

adaptation: changes in organisms that help them survive in an environment

apex predator: an animal that has no natural predators and is at the top of a food chain

Arctic: the region around the North Pole

ecosystem: a community of plants, animals, and other organisms and their environment

fetus: an unborn mammal or other vertebrate that has begun to develop a structure

hibernation: a body's slowing of metabolism and heart rate during times of low access to food

ice floe: a large piece of floating ice

metabolism: a chemical process inside a living thing that turns food into energy

solitary: living alone

stalking: to slowly and quietly follow prey in order to hunt it

LERNER

SOURCE

Expand learning beyond the printed book. Download free, complementary educational resources for this book from our website, www.lerneresource.com.

Learn More about Polar Bears

Books

Castaldo, Nancy F., and Karen de Seve. *Mission: Polar Bear Rescue: All about Polar Bears and How to Save Them*. Washington, DC: National Geographic, 2014. This book shows how people can save polar bears from possible extinction.

Higgins, Nadia. *Deadly Adorable Animals*. Minneapolis: Lerner Publications, 2013. Looks can be deceiving; learn about cute, furry animals that are also fierce predators.

Marsh, Laura F. *Polar Bears*. Washington, DC: National Geographic, 2013. Discover fascinating facts about the polar bear, from how they care for their young to the threats to their environment.

Websites

National Geographic Kids: Polar Bear
http://kids.nationalgeographic.com/animals/polar-bear
This website is home to facts, videos, and games about polar bears, as well as other bears and Arctic animals.

Polar Bears International: Polar Bears for Kids
http://www.polarbearsinternational.org/for-students/polar-bears-for-kids
Get polar bear project ideas, watch tundra webcasts, and participate in the Project Polar Bear Contest to fight climate change.

San Diego Zoo Kids: Polar Bear
http://kids.sandiegozoo.org/animals/mammals/polar-bear
The San Diego Zoo is a portal into the polar bear's world, featuring lots of facts and photos, along with a link to a webcam where fans can watch the zoo's polar bear enclosure.

Index

Arctic region, 9, 11

birds, 8, 14

climate change, 13
coat, 6, 16–17
cubs, 22–23, 25

ecosystem, 12, 14

fat, 8, 14, 17, 22, 24
fights, 26–27
fish, 12

habitat, 8–11

nictitating membrane, 18
North Pole, 10
Norway, 9

paws, 19
predators, 6, 8, 12, 15, 23, 27

sea ice, 4, 11, 13–14
seal, 4–8, 11–12, 14, 18, 20, 27
size, 15

walking hibernation, 24

Photo Acknowledgments

The images in this book are used with the permission of: © jrphoto6/iStock.com, pp. 4, 25 (left); © Maksimilian/Shutterstock.com, p. 5; © Steven J. Kazlowski/Alamy Stock Photo, p. 6; © BMJ/Shutterstock.com, p. 7; © SeppFriedhuber/iStock.com, p. 8; © zanskar/iStock.com, p. 9; © Red Line Editorial, p. 10; © JohnPitcher/iStock.com, pp. 11, 15; © PeterZwitser/iStock.com, pp. 12, 25 (bottom); © Bryan and Cherry Alexander/Science Source, pp. 13, 14; © dagsjo/iStock.com, pp. 16, 29 (top); © ElementalImaging/iStock.com, p. 17; © Jhaviv/iStock.com, p. 18; © ElliotHurwitt/iStock.com, p. 19; © Peter Steffen/DPA/Getty Images, p. 20; © USO/iStock.com, pp. 21, 24, 26; © Kenneth_A_Meisner/iStock.com, p. 22; © 49pauly/iStock.com, p. 23; © Hans-Martin Issler/AP Images, p. 25 (top); © robertharding/Alamy Stock Photo, p. 25 (right); © WorldFoto/Alamy Stock Photo, p. 27; © Vladimir Melnik/Shutterstock.com, p. 29 (middle top); © pomarinus/iStock.com, p. 29 (middle bottom); © Videologia/iStock.com, p. 29 (bottom).

Front Cover: © Mikko Hyvärinen/Shutterstock.com.

Main body text set in Adrianna Regular 14/20.
Typeface provided by Chank.